MEMO

An Autobi

Mem Fox

Contents

For Elaine

My family

Hello! My name is Mem Fox. Let me tell you something about my life and about how I became a writer of children's books.

I was born in Melbourne, Australia on 5 March 1946. My parents are Wilfrid Gordon McDonald Partridge and Nancy Walkden Partridge. I have two younger sisters, Jan and Alison.

Nan & Wilfrid Partridge with Mem, 1946

Family tree

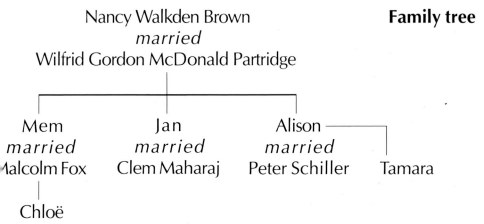

Nancy Walkden Brown
married
Wilfrid Gordon McDonald Partridge

Mem	Jan	Alison
married	*married*	*married*
Malcolm Fox	Clem Maharaj	Peter Schiller Tamara
Chloë		

3

Growing up

When I was six months old my parents went to Africa to work as teachers and missionaries. I grew up in a country now known as Zimbabwe. I was the only white child in my school.

1950

I spoke the local language, *Ndebele*, better than I spoke English. Like the other children in my class I learnt to write by writing letters with my finger, in the dusty, red earth.

1950

However I did not stay at this school long. My parents were told that white children had to go to 'white' schools. This made me very unhappy because I had to wear shoes every day and I had to leave all my friends behind.

1954, aged 8
Rhodesia (now
Zimbabwe)

1956, aged 10
Capetown,
South Africa

1956, aged 10
Rhodesia

1962, aged 16
Rhodesia

1962, aged 16. Mem with
award for winning speech

5

1961, aged 15
Rhodesia

1965, aged 19
Switzerland

Childhood writing

In the end I enjoyed my new school, because I love being with people. English was my favourite subject and my high school English teacher, Miss Smith, was my favourite teacher. She told me I was a good writer. When I was fourteen she asked me to read my story about a cheetah to the whole class. I never forgot that moment. I felt *fantastic!*

n the evenings, my mother, father and I used to write. I wrote my first book when I was ten. At ourteen I wrote a story which filled a whole exercise book. It was about the friendship between a white girl and a black girl. It was so ad, I cried as I wrote it.

At sixteen I wrote the prize-winning speech in a public-speaking competition. It made me feel so great, that I've loved making speeches ever since.

Becoming an actress

left school in 1964. My parents wanted me to go to university but I went to drama school in London instead. I had wanted to be an actress ever since I was thirteen, when I played the part of Alice in the school play *Alice in Wonderland*.

From 1965-68, I learnt how to be an actress. I loved it but decided I preferred writing to acting. So I didn't become an actress after all.

Meeting Malcolm

The best thing about drama school was that I met Malcolm Fox in the cafeteria. Malcolm and I married in 1969. We lived for a while in Africa and England, before coming to Australia in 1970. We have lived in Adelaide ever since. Our only child, Chloë, was born in 1971.

1971, Chloë & Mem

1969, Mem & Malcolm's wedding day

1972, Mem, Malcolm & Chloë

Adult writing

In 1976 I did a course about children's books. For homework, I wrote a story which I called *Hush, the Invisible Mouse.*

Extract from *Hush, the Invisible Mouse* draft

Once there was a mouse. Well, was that special? This one was. Awfully, extra, ultra special. She was the only one of her kind in the whole world. She was what you call unique. Her name was Hush. She was small, quiet, brilliantly clever and she loved adventures. The most important thing about her, the most amazing thing about her, the most unbelievable thing about her was that she was important, amazing and unbelievable. You see, Hush was invisible. You couldn't see her. You could hear her. You could feel her. Sometimes you could even smell her. But you could never actually see her. Amazing! Important! Unbelievable!

My teacher, Felicity Hughes, loved the story and encouraged me to try to have it published. Julie Vivas, an illustrator, did some beautiful pictures for the story, but it was rejected by nine different publishers over five years. I re-wrote it and re-wrote it. I began to think that perhaps I couldn't write after all. Then one day I heard about a new publisher in Adelaide — Omnibus Books — so I made an appointment and took in my story.

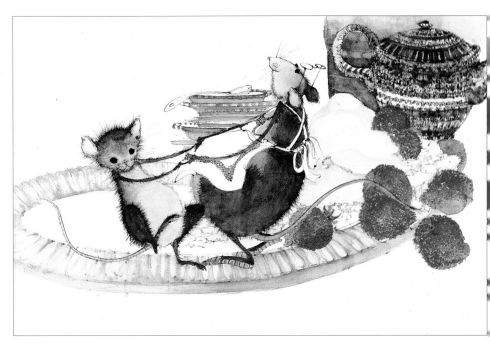

Illustration for *Hush, the Invisible Mouse* by Julie Vivas

Omnibus wanted to publish my book! I was wild with excitement! I changed the mouse to a possum and called the story *Possum Magic*. It was published in 1983 and became the best-selling children's book in the history of Australia. More than 450,000 copies of *Possum Magic* have been sold!

In 1984 *Possum Magic* was short-listed for the Australian Picture Book of the Year Award, but it didn't win and I was devastated. It *did* win Best Children's Book in the 1984 New South Wales Premier's Literary Awards, which cheered me up a little.

I was now a published writer! My second book, *Wilfrid Gordon McDonald Partridge*, was named after my dad. Since then I've written eighteen books, two of them for adults. There are many more to come.

My books have been published in many different countries and in many languages.

My favourite book, of those I've written, is *Koala Lou*. I think it's because Koala Lou is really me. I'm the oldest child in my family and I remember feeling jealous and left out when my sisters were born. Also, like Koala Lou, I came second in an important competition (the Children's Book Awards), but my mother still loved me in spite of the fact that I didn't win.

t took me two years to write *Koala Lou* even
hough it's only 410 words. I did forty-nine
drafts for *Koala Lou* before the book was ready
o be published.

> But it was her mother who loved her most of
> all. A hundred times a day she would laugh
> and shake her head and say, "Koala Lou, I DO
> love you!"

Extract from draft 34 of
Koala Lou and the final text

Why I write

write for many reasons. If an idea jumps into
my head I just have to write it down. I write
because people seem to love my books. I earn
quite a bit from my books, which is another reason
or re-drafting again and again.

My ideas come from events that happen to me in real life. I read a lot, which helps me to know how to write as well as what to write about. My best advice for anyone who'd like to be a writer is: READ!!

I always write my early drafts in pencil, but I transfer the story to a computer for the final, polishing drafts. I usually write late at night, at weekends and on my holidays.

My life now

I teach at Flinders University, in South Australia. Malcolm works there too, as a drama lecturer. Chloë hopes to become a journalist. We live with two little dogs, an aloof cat and two goldfish given to us by Chloë when she left home.

In 1991, I won two awards — the Dromkeen Medal, for outstanding contributions to Australian children's literature; and an Advance Australia Award for distinguished services to literature.

I feel really pleased with my life so far. I guess the only bad thing about it is my feeling tired most of the time because I'm so busy.

Mem Fox,
1991

The future . . .

I have only three ambitions: to live by the sea
to publish a novel for adults, and to write such
a great book for kids that it wins the Australian
Picture Book of the Year Award. My fingers are
tightly crossed!